BEST
SWEETS
& TREATS
FOR TWO

FAST AND FOOLPROOF RECIPES
FOR ONE, TWO, OR A FEW

LAURA ARNOLD

THE COUNTRYMAN PRESS

A DIVISION OF W. W. NORTON & COMPANY

INDEPENDENT PUBLISHERS SINCE 1923

For information about permission to reproduce selections from this book, write to Permissions, The Countryman Press, 500 Fifth Avenue, New York, NY 10110

For information about special discounts for bulk purchases, please contact W. W. Norton Special Sales at specialsales@wwnorton.com or 800-233-4830

The Countryman Press
www.countrymanpress.com

A division of W. W. Norton & Company, Inc.,
500 Fifth Avenue, New York, NY 10110
www.wwnorton.com

978-1-68268-034-6 (pbk.)

10 9 8 7 6 5 4 3 2 1

BEST SWEETS & TREATS FOR TWO

FOR MY MOM—
THANKS FOR BEING
THE SOUS-CHEF OF MY LIFE

BEST SWEETS & TREATS FOR TWO
CONTENTS

Introduction

Maybe it's 10:00 p.m. and your late-night chocolate craving has hit, or maybe it's Saturday after a great cookout and you want something sweet to finish the meal—but you don't have anything on hand. So what do you think? *I hate baking—I don't want to pull out all of the measuring cups and spoons. Desserts take too much time.* But it doesn't always have to be that way. With these recipes, you can have an easy and delicious dessert for two on the table in no time.

Whether baking is your forte or you find it a struggle, what's great about these desserts is how easy they are to make. The key is to follow the steps, relax, and use store-bought solutions to help you along the way. Substitute pre-cut frozen strawberries for fresh to take away the hassle of cleaning and chopping the fruit. Use quick baking mixes to make biscuits or cakes, and add your own touch with fresh ingredients and new spices. These are just some of the sweet solutions provided in these recipes.

And with a serving size of two, dessert becomes even easier to prepare. At a dinner party, smaller desserts can be better—they allow guests to consider dessert optional or to have a smaller serving if they are feeling full or watching what they eat. For larger gatherings, you can serve these desserts in shot glasses or on bread-and-butter-size plates as a fun way to provide a smaller portion—and with less cooking for you. Even if you are just having a quiet night at home, small portions can be welcome after large meals.

Here, you will find easy cookie, cake, ice cream, tart, and crumble recipes—you will discover new favorites that friends and family will be asking for every time they come over for dinner. The sweet tooth will come out and request the Warm Skillet Cookie on movie nights, quick Strawberry Shortcake after summer meals, and Berry Crumble after a long day at work. These recipes will have you saying "yes" to making dessert.

Baking Mixes and Equipment

To make great use of this book, keep your favorite store-bought cake mixes, brownie mixes, frozen fruit, chocolate chips, and pie doughs on hand. These store-bought items will become your best friends when tackling quick desserts that taste 100 percent homemade. What is great about *Best Sweets & Treats for Two* is that most of these cake and brownie recipes call for half a box of store-bought cake or brownie mix (1½ to 2 cups of store-bought mix from a 15.25–ounce box of cake mix or an 18.3–ounce box of brownie mix)—which means that you always have half a box of cake or brownie mix left over to make another dessert the next night or week. Be sure to store your leftover dry boxed mixes in a zip-top bag in the freezer before using again.

With baking for two comes a recipe yield that is a quarter or half the size of a regular dessert recipe. Fewer ingredients means it is necessary to bake in smaller vessels, so having the right equipment is essential. For these recipes to be most successful, you will need:

- Mini muffin tins and full-size muffin tins
- 8-inch cast-iron skillet
- 4-ounce and 8-ounce ramekins or mason jars
- 9- by 5-inch standard loaf pan and 6- by 3.5-inch mini loaf pan
- 8-inch square baking dish

The best part about these recipes is that they are quick and easy. Most of the treats can also be frozen and reheated in the oven, so dessert never ends!

CHAPTER ONE
COOKIES

Skillet Cookie

Warm and gooey, you will be craving this cookie at any time of the day.

Prep time: 15 minutes   Cook time: 20 minutes   Makes one 8-inch cookie

8 tablespoons (1 stick) unsalted butter, softened

⅓ cup granulated sugar

⅓ cup light brown sugar

1 large egg

½ teaspoon vanilla extract

½ teaspoon salt

1 cup all-purpose flour

½ teaspoon baking soda

1 cup semisweet chocolate chips

½ cup walnuts, chopped (optional)

Vanilla ice cream, for serving

Preheat the oven to 350°F. Beat the butter, sugar, and brown sugar together using a hand mixer or stand mixer until light and fluffy. Add the egg, vanilla, and salt and beat until just combined. Add the flour and baking soda and mix until combined. Fold in the chocolate chips and walnuts. Pour the batter into an 8-inch cast-iron skillet. Place the skillet in the oven and bake for 15 to 17 minutes, until golden brown and gooey in the center. Remove from the oven and allow to cool for 5 to 10 minutes. Serve with vanilla ice cream.

Chocolate Hazelnut Cookies

What could be better? Everyone's favorite chocolate hazelnut spread now in a cookie—dig in!

Prep time: 15 minutes   Cook time: 15 minutes   Makes 1 dozen cookies

4 tablespoons (½ stick) unsalted butter, softened

3 tablespoons brown sugar

1 large egg

¼ cup chocolate hazelnut spread

1¼ cup all-purpose flour

½ teaspoon baking soda

¼ cup shelled hazelnuts or walnuts, chopped (optional)

Preheat the oven to 350°F. Line a baking sheet with parchment paper. Beat the butter and sugar together using a hand mixer or stand mixer until light and fluffy. Add the egg and beat to combine. Add the chocolate hazelnut spread and fold with a spatula to combine. Add the flour and baking soda and mix to combine. Fold in the hazelnuts or walnuts if using. Drop the dough onto parchment paper, leaving 1 inch between each cookie. Bake for 8 to 10 minutes or until the cookies are set, but still soft in the center. Remove the baking sheet from the oven and transfer to a baking rack. Allow the cookies to cool on the baking sheet for 2 minutes, then transfer the cookies to the baking rack to cool completely.

Oatmeal Chocolate Chip Pecan Cookies

Combine oats and your favorite nut for this easy cookie. Anything you have in your pantry will have you making dessert in no time!

Prep time: 15 minutes   Cook time: 15 minutes   Makes 1 dozen cookies

8 tablespoons (1 stick) unsalted butter, softened

⅓ cup granulated sugar

⅓ cup brown sugar

1 large egg

½ teaspoon vanilla extract

½ teaspoon salt

1 cup all-purpose flour

½ teaspoon baking soda

½ cup old-fashioned oats

1 cup semisweet chocolate chips

½ cup pecans or other nuts, chopped

Preheat the oven to 350°F. Line a baking sheet with parchment paper. Beat the butter, sugar, and brown sugar together using a hand mixer or stand mixer until light and fluffy. Add the egg, vanilla, and salt and beat to combine. Add the flour and baking soda and mix until combined. Add the oats, chocolate chips, and nuts and fold to combine with a spatula. Drop the dough onto parchment paper, leaving 1 inch between each cookie. Bake for 8 to 10 minutes, or until the cookies are just set. Remove the baking sheet from the oven and transfer to a baking rack and allow the cookies to cool for 2 minutes on the baking sheet. Transfer the cookies to the baking rack and allow to cool completely.

Blondie Brownie Swirl

Why decide between cookies and brownies when you can have both in one bar! This recipe is easy, using your favorite boxed brownie mix.

Prep time: 20 minutes   Cook time: 50 minutes   Makes 8 bars

FOR THE BROWNIE BATTER

2 cups of your favorite boxed brownie mix

2 large eggs

2 tablespoons milk

4 tablespoons (½ stick) unsalted butter, melted

FOR THE COOKIE BATTER

8 tablespoons (1 stick) unsalted butter, softened

⅓ cup granulated sugar

⅓ cup light brown sugar

1 large egg

½ teaspoon vanilla extract

½ teaspoon salt

1 cup all-purpose flour

½ teaspoon baking soda

1 cup semisweet chocolate chips

To make the brownie batter: Preheat the oven to 350°F. Grease an 8-inch square baking dish with cooking spray. Combine all brownie ingredients and mix until smooth. Add the brownie mixture to the prepared baking dish and smooth.

To make the cookie batter: Beat the butter, sugar, and light brown sugar together using a hand mixer or stand mixer and beat until light and fluffy. Add the egg, vanilla, and salt and beat to combine. Add the flour and baking soda and mix until combined. Add the chocolate chips and fold to combine with a spatula. Dollop the cookie dough by the tablespoon over the pan of brownies. Using the tip of a knife, make gentle swirls to incorporate the cookie dough into the brownie mix, but do not over-swirl. Place in the oven and bake for 45 to 50 minutes, until an inserted toothpick comes out clean. If the top is getting too brown, shield with a sheet of foil on top and continue to bake. Remove from the oven and allow to cool for 10 to 15 minutes on a baking rack. Cut and serve.

Apple Pie Cookies

This recipe is perfect for fall. Skip making a whole apple pie and make these cinnamon apple cookies instead.

Prep time: 15 minutes   Cook time: 15 minutes   Makes 1 dozen cookies

- 8 tablespoons (1 stick) unsalted butter, softened
- 1/3 cup granulated sugar
- 1/3 cup dark brown sugar
- 1 large egg
- 1/2 teaspoon vanilla extract
- 1/2 teaspoon salt
- 1 cup all-purpose flour
- 1/2 teaspoon cinnamon
- 1/2 teaspoon baking soda
- 1/2 cup old-fashioned oats
- 1 apple, peeled, finely diced
- 1/2 cup walnuts, chopped (optional)

Preheat the oven to 350°F. Line a baking sheet with parchment paper. Beat the butter, sugar, and brown sugar together using a hand mixer or stand mixer until light and fluffy. Add the egg, vanilla, and salt and beat to combine. Add the flour, baking soda, and cinnamon and beat to combine. Add the oats, apple, and walnuts and fold to combine using a rubber spatula. Drop the dough 1 inch apart on the parchment paper. Bake for 8 to 12 minutes, until golden brown. Remove the baking sheet from the oven and transfer to a baking rack. Allow the cookies to cool on the baking sheet for 2 minutes, then transfer the cookies to the baking rack to cool completely.

Coconut Chocolate Macaroons

Just like a chocolate coconut candy bar, these macaroons are addictive. They also make the perfect gift.

Prep time: 15 minutes   Cook time: 30 minutes   Makes 1 dozen cookies

2 cups sweetened shredded coconut

½ cup sweetened condensed milk

½ teaspoon vanilla extract

2 large egg whites

¼ teaspoon salt

¼ cup semisweet or bittersweet chocolate

Preheat the oven to 350°F. Line a baking sheet with parchment paper. Combine the coconut, sweetened condensed milk, and vanilla. In a separate bowl, whip the egg whites and salt using a hand mixer or stand mixer on high speed until stiff peaks form, about 5 minutes. Add the egg whites to the coconut mixture and gently fold to combine. Drop the macaroons by the tablespoon 1 inch apart onto the parchment paper. Bake for 20 to 25 minutes, until golden brown. Remove from the oven to a baking rack and allow the macaroons to cool completely. Meanwhile, heat the chocolate in the microwave in a microwave-safe bowl for 15-second intervals, stirring in between each interval until smooth and melted. Drizzle over the cooled cookies and allow the chocolate to set.

Peanut Butter Cookies

A homemade classic anyone will love. Add chocolate for even more decadence.

Prep time: 15 minutes   Cook time: 15 minutes   Makes 1 dozen cookies

4 tablespoons (½ stick) unsalted butter, softened

⅓ cup granulated sugar

⅓ cup light brown sugar

⅓ cup creamy peanut butter

1 large egg

½ teaspoon vanilla extract

½ teaspoon salt

1 cup all-purpose flour

½ teaspoon baking soda

1 cup semisweet chocolate chips (optional)

Preheat the oven to 350°F. Line a baking sheet with parchment paper. Beat the butter, sugar, and brown sugar together using a hand mixer or stand mixer until light and fluffy. Add the peanut butter and beat to combine. Add the egg, vanilla, and salt and beat to combine. Add the flour and baking soda and beat until just combined. Drop the dough by the tablespoon 1 inch apart onto the parchment paper. Roll the dough into balls. Press the back of a fork into the top of the dough to flatten. Bake for 10 to 12 minutes, until golden brown. Remove the baking sheet from the oven to a baking rack and allow the cookies to cool for 2 minutes on the baking sheet, then transfer the cookies to the baking rack to cool completely.

To add chocolate, place the chocolate chips in a microwave-safe bowl and microwave at 15-second intervals, stirring in between each interval, until smooth. Dip half of a cookie into the melted chocolate and place on a greased baking rack until the chocolate sets. Repeat with the remaining cookies.

Double Chocolate Chip Cookies

Break out the cocoa powder—if you are a chocolate lover these cookies will be a dangerous craving.

Prep time: 15 minutes   Cook time: 15 minutes   Makes 1 dozen cookies

8 tablespoons (1 stick) unsalted butter, softened

⅓ cup granulated sugar

⅓ cup light brown sugar

1 large egg

½ teaspoon vanilla extract

½ teaspoon salt

3 tablespoons unsweetened cocoa powder

1 cup all-purpose flour

½ teaspoon baking soda

1 cup semisweet chocolate chips

Preheat the oven to 350°F. Line a baking sheet with parchment paper. Beat the butter, sugar, and light brown sugar together using a hand mixer or stand mixer until light and fluffy. Add the egg, vanilla extract, and salt and beat to combine. Add the cocoa powder and beat to combine. Add the flour and baking soda and beat to combine. Add the chocolate chips and fold to combine using a rubber spatula. Drop the dough by the tablespoon 1 inch apart on the parchment paper. Bake for 8 to 12 minutes, until just set. Remove the baking sheet from the oven to a baking rack and allow the cookies to cool on the baking sheet for 2 minutes, then transfer the cookies to the baking rack to cool completely.

Pumpkin Cookies

These are great treats for fall. Using pumpkin puree keeps them moist and full of pumpkin flavor.

Prep time: 15 minutes   Cook time: 15 minutes   Makes 1 dozen cookies

4 tablespoons (½ stick) unsalted butter, softened

⅓ cup granulated sugar

⅓ cup light brown sugar

1 large egg

½ teaspoon vanilla extract

½ teaspoon salt

½ cup pumpkin puree (not pumpkin pie mix)

¼ teaspoon cinnamon

1¼ cups all-purpose flour

½ teaspoon baking soda

Preheat the oven to 350°F. Line a baking sheet with parchment paper. Beat the butter, sugar, and brown sugar together using a hand mixer or stand mixer until light and fluffy. Add the egg, vanilla, and salt and beat until combined. Add the pumpkin puree and cinnamon and beat until just incorporated. Add the flour and baking soda and beat until just combined. Drop the dough by the tablespoon 1 inch apart. Bake for 8 to 12 minutes, until golden brown. Remove the baking sheet from the oven to a baking rack and allow the cookies to cool on the pan for 2 minutes, then transfer the cookies to the baking rack to cool completely.

Ginger Cookies

Perfect for an afternoon coffee or tea break, these ginger spice cookies have a combination of spices that you will want with after-dinner coffee every night.

Prep time: 15 minutes   Cook time: 15 minutes   Makes 1 dozen cookies

4 tablespoons (½ stick) unsalted butter, softened

½ cup plus 1 cup granulated sugar

1 large egg

½ teaspoon vanilla extract

¼ teaspoon salt

3 tablespoons molasses

1 cup all-purpose flour

½ teaspoon baking soda

1 teaspoon ground ginger

¼ teaspoon cinnamon

⅛ teaspoon ground cloves

Preheat the oven to 350°F. Line a baking sheet with parchment paper. Beat the butter and ½ cup granulated sugar together using a hand mixer or stand mixer until light and fluffy. Add the egg, vanilla, and salt and beat to combine. Add the molasses and beat until combined. Add the flour, baking soda, ginger, cinnamon, and cloves and mix until combined. Add the remaining 1 cup sugar to a baking dish. Roll the dough by the tablespoon into balls. Roll each ball in the sugar to coat and place on the parchment paper. Repeat, spacing the dough 1 inch apart. Bake for 8 to 12 minutes, until golden brown. Remove the baking sheet from the oven to a baking rack and allow the cookies to cool on the pan for 2 minutes, then transfer the cookies to the baking rack to cool completely.

CHAPTER TWO

SWEET
SMALL
BITES

Cheesecake Bites with Blueberries

Have cheesecake in no time and without the stress! Pair with your favorite fruit toppings for a perfect summer dessert. These can be stored in the freezer for a no-hassle treat all week.

Prep time: 15 minutes   Cook time: 15 minutes   Makes 6 mini cheesecakes

1½ cups vanilla wafer cookies, crushed

2 tablespoons unsalted butter, melted

One 8-ounce package cream cheese, softened

⅓ cup granulated sugar

1 large egg

½ teaspoon vanilla extract

½ cup blueberries

½ cup blueberry preserves

Preheat the oven to 350°F. Line 6 wells of a muffin tin with liners. Combine the crushed cookies and melted butter in a bowl. Divide the crushed cookies between the lined muffin wells and press down into the bottom of the tin. Combine the cream cheese and sugar and beat using a hand mixer or stand mixer until light and fluffy. Add the egg and vanilla extract and beat until just combined. Divide between the prepared muffin wells (they should be ⅔ full) and bake for 12 to 15 minutes, until just set but with a slight jiggle in the center. Remove from the oven and transfer to a cooling rack to cool completely. Combine the blueberries and blueberry preserves. Spoon blueberry mixture on top of the cooled cheesecakes or serve on the side.

Chocolate Truffles

This anytime chocolate treat looks and tastes decadent but is so easy to make. Perfect for a date night in or a special occasion—everyone will be asking you for this recipe.

Prep time: 30 minutes   Cook time: 45 minutes   Makes 20 truffles

1 cup semisweet chocolate chips

1 cup bittersweet chocolate chips

½ cup heavy cream

½ teaspoon vanilla extract

¼ teaspoon salt

½ cup cocoa powder

Combine the semisweet chocolate chips, bittersweet chocolate chips, and heavy cream in a microwave-safe bowl. Microwave in 15-second intervals, stirring in between each interval until chocolate is smooth. Add the vanilla and salt and stir to combine. Pour the mixture into a loaf pan, place in the freezer, and allow to set for 20 minutes. Scoop the chocolate into 1-inch balls using a cookie scoop or melon baller and roll with hands until smooth. Place on a baking sheet. Repeat until all the chocolate is rolled. Chill in the refrigerator or freezer for another 10 minutes. Fill a shallow bowl with the cocoa powder. Remove the truffles from the refrigerator and roll in cocoa powder. Store in the refrigerator or freezer until ready to serve. Serve at room temperature.

S'mores Bark

Bring the campfire indoors with this chocolate treat. Add your favorite toppings to customize your s'mores candy bark.

Prep time: 10 minutes   Cook time: 40 minutes   Makes 2 to 4 servings

Two 4-ounce bittersweet chocolate bars

One 4-ounce white chocolate bar

½ cup graham crackers, crushed into small pieces

½ cup mini marshmallows

½ cup walnuts, roughly chopped (optional)

Flaky sea salt, for garnish (optional)

Line a baking sheet with wax paper. Place the bittersweet chocolate in one microwave-safe bowl, and the white chocolate in another microwave-safe bowl. Microwave the chocolates at 15-second intervals, stirring in between each interval, until smooth and melted. Pour the bittersweet chocolate onto the prepared baking sheet in a smooth, even layer, about ¼-inch thick. Drizzle the white chocolate over the bittersweet chocolate and make swirls using the tip of a knife or skewer. Evenly sprinkle the graham crackers, marshmallows, walnuts, and sea salt over the top. Allow to set in the freezer for 30 minutes or until firm. Break into pieces.

Red Velvet Cake Bites

Using store-bought red velvet cake or boxed red velvet cake mix makes this recipe effortless. Swap out your favorite flavor of cake for any occasion.

Prep time: 45 minutes   Cook time: 1 hour   Makes 15 cake bites

Cooking spray, for greasing

2 cups store-bought red velvet cake mix or 4 cups crumbled store-bought cake

1 large egg (if using cake mix)

½ cup water (if using cake mix)

3 tablespoons vegetable oil (if using cake mix)

½ cup store-bought vanilla frosting

1½ cups white chocolate chips or white candy coating

Red sugar sprinkles, for garnish

If using cake mix, preheat the oven to 350°F. Grease an 8-inch square baking pan with cooking spray. Line a baking sheet with wax paper. Combine the cake mix, egg, water, and vegetable oil in a large bowl and mix using a hand mixer or stand mixer for 2 minutes until smooth. Pour into the prepared baking pan and bake for 30 to 35 minutes, until an inserted toothpick comes out clean. Remove from the oven and transfer to a baking rack to cool completely.

Break the prepared or store-bought cake into fine crumbs and place in a bowl. Add the frosting and beat using a hand mixer or stand mixer until just combined. Form the cake into 1-inch balls using a cookie scoop and place on the prepared baking sheet. Freeze for 10 minutes. Meanwhile, in a microwave-safe bowl, melt the chocolate or candy coating in the microwave, stirring at 15-second intervals. Roll the cake balls in the chocolate until coated, lift out of the chocolate with a fork, allowing excess to drip off, and place back on the wax paper. Repeat with remaining cake balls, sprinkle with red sprinkles, and freeze another 15 minutes until set.

Caramel Peanut Popcorn

Movie night just got even better with this toffee popcorn. Easy and addictive, this treat will be gone before you know it.

Prep time: 10 minutes   **Cook time: 15 minutes**   **Makes 4 cups**

Cooking spray, for greasing

4 cups butter popcorn, popped

¾ cup honey roasted peanuts

1½ cups chewy caramel candies

1 teaspoon sea salt or kosher salt

Grease two baking sheets with cooking spray. Toss the popcorn and peanuts together and spread out onto the two baking sheets. Microwave the chewy caramels in 30-second intervals, stirring in between each interval until smooth. Pour over popcorn and quickly toss to coat. Sprinkle with sea salt and allow to set, 5 to 10 minutes. Serve.

Tip: Spray your hands and spatula with cooking spray before tossing the popcorn with the melted caramel.

Cookies & Cream Bites

Use your favorite store-bought cookies for this easy homemade dessert.

Prep time: 30 minutes   Cook time: 20 minutes   Makes 1 dozen bites

12 chocolate crème cookies

½ cup store-bought vanilla or chocolate frosting

1 cup milk chocolate chips or chocolate candy coating

Line a baking sheet with wax paper. Crush the chocolate crème cookies until finely ground in a food processor or in a zip-top bag using a rolling pin. Transfer the crumbles to a large bowl. Add the vanilla frosting and mix until well combined. Scoop into 1-inch balls using a small cookie scoop or melon baller. Place on the prepared baking sheet and freeze for 10 minutes, or until set. Meanwhile, in a microwave-safe bowl, melt the chocolate in the microwave in 15-second intervals, stirring in between until smooth. With a fork, dip the cookie balls into the chocolate and coat completely. Remove the balls from the chocolate, allowing excess chocolate to drip off. Return to the wax paper and freeze another 10 minutes until set.

Lemon Tartlets

Store-bought lemon curd makes lemon tartlets come together in a pinch! Pucker up for this citrus surprise.

Prep time: 25 minutes   Cook time: 30 minutes   Makes 1 dozen bites

FOR THE TARTLETS

¾ cup shortbread cookies or vanilla wafer cookies, finely crushed

½ cup almonds, finely ground

½ teaspoon salt

4 tablespoons (½ stick) unsalted butter, melted

One 10-ounce jar lemon curd

Lemon zest, for serving (optional)

Poppy seeds, for serving (optional)

FOR THE WHIPPED CREAM

½ cup heavy whipping cream, chilled

2 tablespoons powdered sugar

To make the tartlets: Preheat the oven to 350°F. Line a mini muffin tin with mini muffin liners. Combine crushed cookies, almonds, salt, and butter. Spoon 1 to 2 tablespoons of the crust into each lined muffin well and press down. Bake for 6 to 8 minutes, until golden brown. Remove from the oven to a baking rack and allow to cool completely. Spoon 2 to 3 tablespoons of lemon curd over each crust and refrigerate for at least 15 minutes—preferably longer.

To make the whipped cream: Whip heavy cream using a hand mixer or stand mixer for 5 minutes on medium speed until soft peaks form. Add powdered sugar and continue whipping another 2 to 3 minutes until medium peaks form. Spoon on top of the lemon tarts. Sprinkle with lemon zest and poppy seeds if desired.

Chocolate Peanut Butter Rice Cereal Bars

Your favorite treat from childhood but with a new gourmet look. Combine your favorite cereals with marshmallows for a quick weeknight dessert.

Prep time: 15 minutes   Cook time: 15 minutes   Makes 8 treats

Cooking spray for greasing

3 tablespoons unsalted butter

One 10.5-ounce bag mini marshmallows

⅓ cup creamy peanut butter

6 cups chocolate rice cereal

Grease an 8-inch square baking pan with cooking spray. Melt the butter in a large pot over medium heat. Add the marshmallows and cook for 5 to 7 minutes, until smooth and melted. Add the peanut butter and stir to combine. Add the chocolate rice cereal and stir to coat completely. Transfer to the prepared baking dish and lightly press into an even layer. Allow to cool, 5 to 10 minutes. Cut into bars.

German Chocolate Brownie Bites

Make your own brownie bites and garnish with your favorite cake toppings. These German chocolate bites have a thick caramel icing with walnuts and coconut.

Prep time: 25 minutes   Cook time: 30 minutes   Makes 2 dozen mini bites

FOR THE BROWNIES

Cooking spray, for greasing

2 cups store-bought brownie mix

2 large eggs

2 tablespoons water

¼ cup vegetable oil

½ cup walnuts, roughly chopped

TO ASSEMBLE

¼ cup store-bought caramel sauce

3 to 4 tablespoons powdered sugar

1 to 2 tablespoons milk (optional)

⅓ cup sweetened shredded coconut

To make the brownies: Preheat the oven to 325°F for a coated or dark pan or 350°F for a light metal pan. Grease a mini muffin tin with cooking spray. Combine all of the brownie ingredients. Divide the batter evenly between the prepared muffin wells and bake for 12 to 15 minutes, or until set. Remove from the oven to a baking rack and allow to cool in the tin for 10 minutes, then remove the brownies from the tin and allow to cool completely.

To assemble the brownies: Whisk the caramel sauce and powdered sugar until thickened but smooth. Add a little milk if the icing becomes too thick. Drizzle brownie bites with caramel icing and sprinkle with coconut.

Turtle Pretzel Crunch

You will be addicted to this snack by the end of the first batch—swirls of caramel and chocolate combined with the crunch of pretzels and pecans create a treat that will be gone in no time.

Prep time: 15 minutes   Cook time: 15 minutes   Makes 2 cups

2½ cups small pretzel twists

1 cup chewy caramels

1 cup pecans

½ cup bittersweet chocolate chips

½ cup white chocolate chips

Line a baking sheet with wax paper. Spread the pretzels on the baking sheet in an even layer. Add the caramels, bittersweet chocolate chips, and white chocolate chips to three different microwave-safe bowls. Microwave at 15-second intervals, stirring each interval, until melted and smooth. Drizzle the caramel over the pretzels. Sprinkle with the pecans. Finally, drizzle with the bittersweet and white chocolate. Allow to set in the freezer for 10 to 15 minutes. Break into pieces and enjoy.

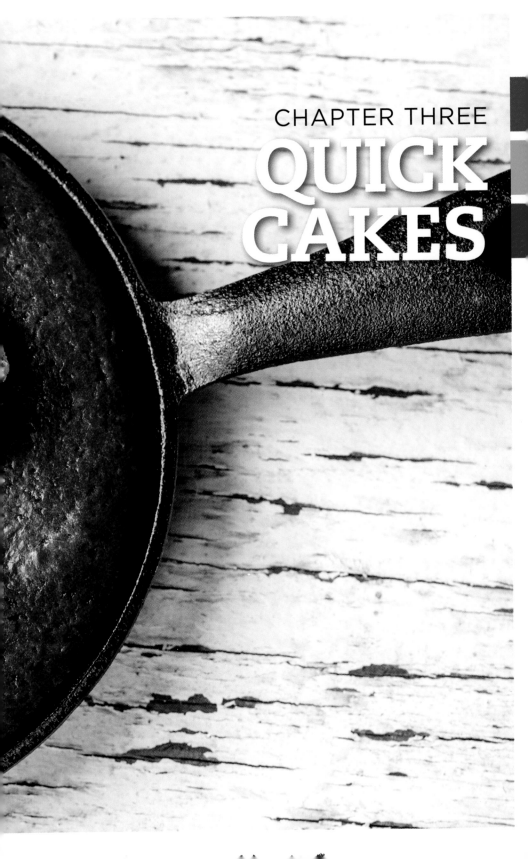

CHAPTER THREE

QUICK CAKES

Cinnamon Streusel Cake

Perfect for breakfast, brunch, or an afternoon snack, this classic cinnamon streusel cake is made with yellow cake mix for an easy store-bought solution.

Prep time: 15 minutes   Cook time: 40 minutes   Makes 2 mini loaves

1½ cups store-bought yellow cake mix

1 large egg plus 1 large egg yolk

½ cup water

3 tablespoons unsalted butter, melted

½ cup dark brown sugar

½ cup all-purpose flour

½ teaspoon cinnamon

3 tablespoons unsalted butter, chilled, diced

1 cup powdered sugar

2–3 tablespoons milk

Preheat the oven to 350°F. Grease two mini loaf pans with cooking spray. Combine the cake mix, egg, egg yolk, water, and melted butter using a hand mixer or a stand mixer until smooth, about 2 minutes. Combine dark brown sugar, flour, cinnamon, and chilled butter in another bowl. Work butter with fingers or the prongs of a fork until pea-sized crumbles form. Divide half of the cake batter between the mini loaf pans. Sprinkle the brown sugar mixture over the cake batter and top with remaining half of cake batter. Bake for 20 to 25 minutes or until an inserted toothpick comes out clean. Remove and allow to cool on a baking rack for 10 minutes. Remove cake from the pan and allow to cool completely on the rack.

Rocky Road
Cake Bars

Transform the classic ice cream flavor into cake bars. The toppings of Rocky Road ice cream make for fun, rich, brownie-like treats.

Prep time: 20 minutes   Cook time: 35 minutes   Makes 8 bars

FOR THE CAKE

Cooking spray for greasing

1½ cups store-bought chocolate cake mix

1 large egg plus 2 large egg yolks

½ cup whole milk

3 tablespoons butter, melted

TO ASSEMBLE

½ can chocolate icing

2 tablespoons powdered sugar

½ teaspoon vanilla extract

1–2 tablespoons milk (optional)

½ cup store-bought caramel sauce, warmed

1 cup mini marshmallows

½ cup mini chocolate chips

½ cup pecans, roughly chopped

To make the cake: Preheat oven to 350°F. Grease an 8-inch square baking pan with cooking spray. Combine all of the cake ingredients and beat using a hand mixer or a stand mixer until smooth, about 2 minutes. Transfer to the prepared baking pan. Bake for 20 to 25 minutes, or until an inserted toothpick comes out clean. Remove from the oven and transfer to a baking rack and allow to cool completely.

To assemble: Whisk together the icing, powdered sugar, and vanilla. If the icing becomes too thick, add a couple of tablespoons of milk. Once the cake has cooled, spread the icing evenly over the top. Drizzle with caramel sauce and sprinkle with marshmallows, chocolate chips, and pecans. Cut into bars and serve.

Tip: If you want, pop the finished cake under the broiler for 1 minute to toast the marshmallows and melt the chocolate. Serve with ice cream for an outrageous dessert!

Toffee Walnut Skillet Brownie

Eat this gooey brownie straight from the oven. Topped with vanilla ice cream, it makes the perfect date night treat. Add your favorite nut or candy mix-ins to fit any occasion.

Prep time: 15 minutes   Cook time: 30 minutes   Makes one 8-inch brownie

2 cups store-bought brownie mix

2 large eggs

2 tablespoons milk

½ cup vegetable oil

½ cup bittersweet chocolate chips

½ cup toffee bits

½ cup walnuts, roughly chopped

Vanilla ice cream, for serving

Preheat the oven to 350°F. Combine the brownie mix, eggs, milk, and vegetable oil. Stir in the chocolate chips, toffee bits, and walnuts. Pour into an 8-inch cast-iron skillet and bake for 25 to 30 minutes, until the edges are set and the middle is almost set but still gooey. Remove from the oven, top with vanilla ice cream, and serve.

Strawberry Shortcake

Prep time: 15 minutes   Cook time: 30 minutes   Makes 4 servings

FOR THE STRAWBERRIES

1 cup strawberries, hulled and thinly sliced

3 tablespoons granulated sugar

Store-bought or homemade whipped cream (page 49), for serving

FOR THE BISCUITS

1 cup baking mix (such as Bisquick)

⅓ cup milk

2 tablespoons granulated sugar

2 tablespoons unsalted butter, melted

½ orange, zested

To prepare the strawberries: Combine the strawberries and sugar and allow to macerate until the strawberries release juices, about 30 minutes.

To make the biscuits: Preheat the oven to 425°F. Line a baking sheet with parchment paper. Combine all of the biscuit ingredients until a soft dough forms. Drop the dough into 4 biscuits onto the prepared baking sheet. Bake for 10 to 12 minutes, until golden brown and fluffy. Remove from the oven and allow to cool slightly.

To serve: Split the biscuits in half and spoon over strawberries and whipped cream.

Peanut Butter Chocolate Cupcakes

A favorite combination, these chocolate cupcakes have a peanut butter surprise inside!

Prep time: 25 minutes   Cook time: 40 minutes   Makes 1 dozen cupcakes

FOR THE CAKE

1½ cups store-bought chocolate cake mix

1 large egg plus 1 large egg yolk

½ cup milk

3 tablespoons vegetable oil

FOR THE FILLING

¾ cup store-bought vanilla frosting

¼ cup creamy peanut butter

FOR THE GANACHE

¼ cup heavy cream

5 ounces semisweet chocolate chips

To make the cake: Preheat oven to 350°F. Line a 12-cup muffin tin with muffin liners. Combine the cake ingredients and beat using a hand mixer or stand mixer for 2 minutes until smooth. Fill the muffin wells ⅔ full. Bake for 20 to 25 minutes, until an inserted toothpick comes out clean. Remove from the oven to a baking rack and allow to cool 10 minutes in the pan. Then transfer the cupcakes from the tin to the baking rack to cool completely.

To make the filling and ganache: Combine the vanilla frosting and peanut butter. Place the mixture into a piping bag or a zip-top bag fitted with a pastry tip. Bring the heavy cream to a simmer in a medium saucepan over medium heat. Pour over chocolate chips, allow to stand for 5 minutes, then stir to combine. Allow to cool until thickened. Poke the pastry tip into the top of the cooled cupcake and squeeze 1 to 2 tablespoons of peanut butter filling in the center. Spread the chocolate ganache over the top and allow to set.

Tip: If you don't have a pastry tip, poke a hole in the top of the cupcake using a paring knife and then pipe frosting into the center.

Chocolate Zucchini Muffins

Lighten up these muffins by using applesauce instead of oil in the cake mix.

Prep time: 25 minutes   Cook time: 25 minutes   Makes 1 dozen muffins

1½ cups devil's food cake mix

⅓ cup cocoa powder

1 large egg plus 1 large egg yolk

½ cup water

¼ cup applesauce

1 small zucchini, grated

½ cup mini chocolate chips

Preheat the oven to 350°F. Line a 12-cup muffin tin with muffin liners or grease with cooking spray. Combine the cake mix, cocoa powder, egg, egg yolk, water, and applesauce, and beat using a hand mixer or stand mixer for 2 minutes until smooth. Stir in the zucchini and chocolate chips. Divide evenly between lined muffin wells and bake for 20 to 25 minutes, or until an inserted toothpick comes out clean. Remove from the oven and transfer to a baking rack to cool for 10 minutes in the pan, then remove the muffins from the tin to cool completely on a baking rack.

Carrot Cake

Rich cream cheese icing and spices make this loaf cake shine.

Prep time: 20 minutes   Cook time: 40 minutes   Makes 2 mini cakes

FOR THE CAKE

Cooking spray, for greasing

1½ cups yellow cake mix

½ cup water

3 tablespoons unsalted butter, melted

1 teaspoon ground cinnamon

¼ teaspoon ground nutmeg

½ teaspoon vanilla extract

1 large egg plus 1 large egg yolk

¾ cup peeled and grated carrots

½ cup walnuts or almonds, roughly chopped, plus additional for garnish

FOR THE CREAM CHEESE ICING

3 tablespoons unsalted butter, softened

5 ounces cream cheese, softened

½ teaspoon vanilla extract

¾ cup powdered sugar

1 to 2 tablespoons milk (optional)

To make the cake: Preheat the oven to 350°F. Grease a two mini loaf pans with cooking spray. Combine the cake mix, water, butter, cinnamon, nutmeg, vanilla, and egg and egg yolk, and beat using a hand mixer or stand mixer for 2 minutes until smooth. Stir in the carrots and nuts. Pour into the mini loaf pans and bake for 25 to 30 minutes, or until an inserted toothpick comes out clean. Remove the cakes to a baking rack to cool in the pan for 10 minutes. Transfer the cakes to the baking rack to cool completely.

To make the cream cheese icing: Combine the butter, cream cheese, and vanilla and beat using a hand mixer or stand mixer until light and fluffy. Gradually add the powdered sugar until thickened. If the icing becomes too thick, add a couple of tablespoons of milk. Spread the icing over the cooled cakes, and garnish with additional walnuts.

Tip: Because of the cream cheese icing, this cake should be stored in the refrigerator.

Mason Jar Brownies & Cream Layered Cakes

Using mason jars makes it easy to keep these desserts on-hand in the freezer. Use mugs if you don't have mason jars.

Prep time: 20 minutes   Cook time: 5 minutes   Makes two 8-ounce mason jars

½ cup heavy whipping cream

2 tablespoons powdered sugar

½ teaspoon vanilla extract

¼ cup bittersweet chocolate chips, plus additional to garnish

2 to 3 brownies, crumbled

¼ cup walnuts, roughly chopped, plus additional to garnish

Beat the heavy whipping cream using a hand mixer or stand mixer for 4 to 5 minutes, until soft peaks form. Add the sugar and vanilla and continue beating until medium-stiff peaks form, 2 to 3 minutes. In a microwave-safe bowl, melt the chocolate chips in the microwave in 15-second intervals, stirring in between each interval, until smooth. Place half of the brownie crumbles in the bottom of each 8-ounce mason jar or mug. Top with half of the melted chocolate, nuts, and whipped cream. Repeat a second time, ending with the whipped cream, and top with additional melted chocolate and nuts. Serve immediately or store in the refrigerator or freezer. If storing in the freezer, allow to thaw for 15 to 20 minutes before serving.

Tip: This recipe is a great way to use up leftover brownies. For the best flavor, allow mason jars to sit in the refrigerator for a few hours before serving.

Mini Lemon Pound Cakes

Serve this cake with fresh berries or stone fruit and whipped cream for a refreshing dessert.

Prep time: 15 minutes   Cook time: 40 minutes   Makes 2 mini loaves

FOR THE POUND CAKES

Cooking spray, for greasing

8 tablespoons (1 stick) unsalted butter, softened

½ cup granulated sugar

2 large eggs

½ teaspoon vanilla extract

½ teaspoon salt

¾ cup all-purpose flour

½ teaspoon baking powder

1 lemon, juiced

FOR THE GLAZE

1 cup powdered sugar

2 to 3 tablespoons whole milk or heavy cream

Lemon slices or zest, for garnish

To make the pound cakes: Preheat the oven to 350°F. Grease two mini loaf pans with cooking spray. Beat the butter and sugar with a hand mixer or stand mixer until light and fluffy. Add the eggs, vanilla extract, and salt and mix until just combined. Add the flour and baking powder and mix until just combined. Add the lemon juice and mix to combine. Scoop the batter into mini loaf pans and bake for 20 to 25 minutes, until an inserted toothpick comes out clean. Remove from the oven to a baking rack to cool in the pan for 10 minutes. Transfer the cakes from the pan and allow to cool completely.

To make the glaze: Whisk together the powdered sugar and heavy cream until thickened but still able to drizzle. Drizzle over the cooled loaf cakes and garnish with lemon slices or zest.

Tiramisu for Two

The traditional Italian dessert made easy in mugs! Layer the ingredients, refrigerate for a couple of hours, and enjoy.

Prep time: 20 minutes   Cook time: 35 minutes plus refrigeration

Makes 2 mugs

½ cup brewed espresso or coffee

1 cup vanilla wafer cookies

1 cup store-bought or homemade whipped cream (page 49)

¼ cup mascarpone cheese or cream cheese, softened

2 tablespoons cocoa powder

Combine the espresso and vanilla wafer cookies in a baking dish and soak for 5 minutes. Meanwhile, whisk the whipped cream and mascarpone cheese together until smooth. Place a layer of soaked vanilla wafers in the bottom of each mug. Top with the whipped cream mixture. Repeat, ending with the whipped cream mixture. Dust cocoa powder over the top. Cover with plastic wrap and refrigerate for at least 30 minutes, preferably a few hours.

Molten Lava Cakes

Bake these lava cakes in a muffin tin, ramekins, or 4-ounce mason jars. You won't believe how easy this restaurant-style dessert is to make at home!

Prep time: 20 minutes   Cook time: 15 minutes   Makes 6 cakes

Cooking spray, for greasing

4 tablespoons (½ stick) unsalted butter

½ cup semisweet or bittersweet chocolate chips

⅓ cup granulated sugar, plus additional to garnish

6 tablespoons all-purpose flour

¼ teaspoon salt

3 large eggs

Powdered sugar, for garnish

Raspberries, for garnish

Preheat the oven to 350°F. Grease a 6-cup muffin tin with cooking spray. Heat the butter and chocolate in a large heatproof glass bowl set over a saucepan of boiling water. Mix until smooth and combined, then allow to cool slightly. Add the sugar, flour, and salt to the chocolate mixture and whisk to combine. Add one egg at a time to the chocolate mixture and whisk until just combined. Divide the mixture between the muffin wells, filling each cup half full, and place in the oven. Bake for 8 minutes or until the top is set but the center is still gooey. Remove from the oven, allow to cool for 1 minute in the pan, then remove from the pan and serve warm. Garnish with powdered sugar and raspberries.

CHAPTER FOUR

ICE CREAM & PUDDING

Caramel Raisin Bread Pudding

Day-old bread? No worries, this recipe solves that problem! To save time, assemble the night before and bake while eating dinner for the easiest dessert.

Prep time: 45 minutes   Cook time: 50 minutes   Makes 2 servings

1 tablespoon unsalted butter or cooking spray, for greasing

½ loaf of day-old white bread, torn into 1-inch pieces

½ cup raisins

2 large eggs

¾ cup milk

⅓ cup granulated sugar

½ teaspoon vanilla extract

½ teaspoon ground cinnamon

½ cup walnuts (optional)

½ cup store-bought caramel sauce

2 teaspoons rum or bourbon (optional)

Preheat the oven to 350°F. Grease an 8-inch cast-iron skillet with butter or cooking spray. Place the bread in the skillet and sprinkle with raisins. Whisk together the eggs, milk, sugar, vanilla, and cinnamon until well-combined. Pour over the bread mixture in the skillet and press down to submerge the bread in the liquid. Soak for 15 to 30 minutes. Sprinkle on the walnuts, if using. Cover with foil and bake for 20 minutes. Remove the foil and bake for another 10 to 15 minutes, until puffed and golden brown—the center will jiggle slightly. Remove and allow to cool for 15 minutes. Meanwhile, heat the caramel sauce in a saucepan over medium heat. Add rum or bourbon, if desired. Serve with the bread pudding.

Banana Pudding

Banana pudding is always a winner, whether for dessert or even breakfast! Vanilla wafer cookies and bananas keep this dessert simple but decadent. Try chocolate cookies for a new twist.

Prep time: 15 minutes   Cook time: 30 minutes plus refrigeration
Makes 2 servings

One 3.4-ounce package instant vanilla or banana pudding

¼ teaspoon ground cinnamon

1 cup vanilla wafer cookies

2 small bananas, peeled and thinly sliced

1 recipe whipped cream (page 49)

Prepare the vanilla pudding according to package directions. When cooked, stir in the cinnamon. Refrigerate, if necessary, until it reaches room temperature. Place a layer of vanilla wafers in the bottom of two mugs or bowls. Top with a layer of bananas and pudding. Repeat, ending with the pudding on top. Top with whipped cream. Allow to sit in the refrigerator for at least 30 minutes, preferably a few hours.

Tip: To avoid refrigerating for hours, soften the vanilla wafers in 1 cup of milk mixed with ½ teaspoon of vanilla extract and ¼ teaspoon of cinnamon until soft, 8 to 10 minutes. Remove the wafers from the milk, layer with pudding and bananas, and serve.

Lemon Pudding with Graham Cracker Crunch

Lemon pie made easy! Add lemon juice and lemon zest to instant lemon pudding and no one will ever know the difference.

Prep time: 10 minutes   Cook time: 20 minutes   Makes two 8-ounce mason jars

One 3.4-ounce package instant lemon pudding

1 lemon, zested and juiced

¾ cup graham crackers, crushed

2 tablespoons unsalted butter, melted

⅓ cup sliced almonds, crushed

1 recipe whipped cream (page 49)

Lemon zest, for garnish (optional)

Prepare the pudding according to package directions. Cool, if necessary, to room temperature. Stir in the lemon zest and juice. Combine the graham crackers, butter, and almonds. Reserve ¼ cup of the graham cracker mixture for garnish. Press to fill the bottom of each mason jar. Add the pudding and top with whipped cream, reserved graham cracker crunch, and lemon zest. Refrigerate until ready to enjoy.

Lemon Raspberry Frozen Yogurt

No need for an ice cream maker—puree frozen fruit in a blender or food processor to have frozen yogurt in no time.

Prep time: 15 minutes   Cook time: 1 to 2 hours   Makes 2 to 3 servings

2 cups frozen raspberries

¼ cup granulated sugar

2 cups plain yogurt

1 lemon, juiced

1½ cups store-bought or homemade whipped cream (page 49)

Combine the raspberries and sugar in a food processor and blend until smooth. Add the yogurt and lemon juice and blend until smooth. Transfer the mixture to a bowl and fold in the whipped cream. Transfer the yogurt to a loaf pan and freeze for at least 1 to 2 hours, until desired consistency is reached.

Chocolate Caramel Peanut Butter Ice Cream Pops

Swirl peanut butter and caramel ice cream together to create this frozen treat.

Prep time: 15 minutes   Cook time: 1 hour   Makes 4 to 6 pops

1 pint caramel ice cream, slightly softened

½ cup creamy peanut butter

4 popsicle sticks

½ cup bittersweet chocolate chips

¼ cup honey roasted peanuts, chopped

Blend the caramel ice cream and peanut butter together in a blender or food processor. Pour into 4 to 6 popsicle molds and place a popsicle stick in the center of each. Freeze for at least 1 hour. When ready to serve, melt the chocolate chips in a microwave-safe bowl in the microwave in 15-second intervals, stirring until smooth. Remove the pops from the mold, drizzle with chocolate, and sprinkle the peanuts over the pops.

Tip: If you don't have a popsicle mold, use small paper cups instead.

Ice Cream Cookie Sandwiches

Have dessert in seconds with your favorite ice cream and cookie. This is the perfect treat to keep in the freezer year-round.

Prep time: 30 minutes   Cook time: 1 hour   Makes 6 sandwiches

1 recipe Double Chocolate Chip Cookies (page 28)

½ pint mint chocolate chip ice cream, softened

½ pint raspberry ice cream, softened

½ cup pistachios, roughly chopped

½ cup mini chocolate chips

Scoop the ice cream on the inside of one cookie, top with the second cookie, and press together. Roll mint chocolate chip sandwiches in pistachios. Roll raspberry sandwiches in mini chocolate chips. Wrap in foil and freeze until ready to serve.

Blueberry Parfait Popsicles

Your favorite breakfast parfait just became a dessert! Freeze yogurt, fruit, and granola for a delicious afternoon treat.

Prep time: 15 minutes   Cook time: 4 to 6 hours   Makes 4 pops

1½ cups plain yogurt

⅓ cup blueberry preserves

½ cup fresh blueberries or thawed frozen blueberries

½ cup store-bought granola

4 popsicle sticks

Blend the yogurt, preserves, and blueberries together in a blender until smooth. Pour into popsicle molds or paper cups and place popsicle sticks down each center. Sprinkle granola over the top of each popsicle mold and press down gently. Freeze until completely hardened, 4 to 6 hours. When ready to serve, remove the pops from the mold.

Turtle Ice Cream Sundae

Swirls of caramel, chocolate, pecans, and salty pretzels make for an ice cream sundae like no other.

Prep time: 15 minutes   Cook time: 1 hour   Makes 2 servings

2 cups vanilla ice cream, softened

¼ cup chocolate sauce plus additional for garnish

¼ cup caramel sauce plus additional for garnish

½ cup pecans, chopped

½ cup, pretzel twists, crushed, plus additional for garnish

Sea salt, for garnish

Blend the vanilla ice cream, chocolate sauce, and caramel sauce in a blender until smooth. Transfer to a bowl and stir in pecans and pretzels. Transfer to a loaf pan and freeze for at least 1 hour. Remove from the freezer, scoop two scoops into each of two bowls, top with additional chocolate sauce, caramel sauce, crushed pretzels, and sea salt.

Cinnamon Cereal Milk Shake

Steep your favorite cereal in milk, strain, and blend with ice cream for the perfect movie night treat!

Prep time: 5 minutes   Cook time: 10 minutes   Makes 2 milkshakes

¾ cup milk

1 cup cinnamon sugar cereal

3 cups vanilla ice cream, softened

Combine the milk and cinnamon sugar cereal and allow to steep for 10 minutes. Strain the milk through a mesh sieve and discard the cereal. Blend the milk and ice cream together in a blender until smooth. Serve.

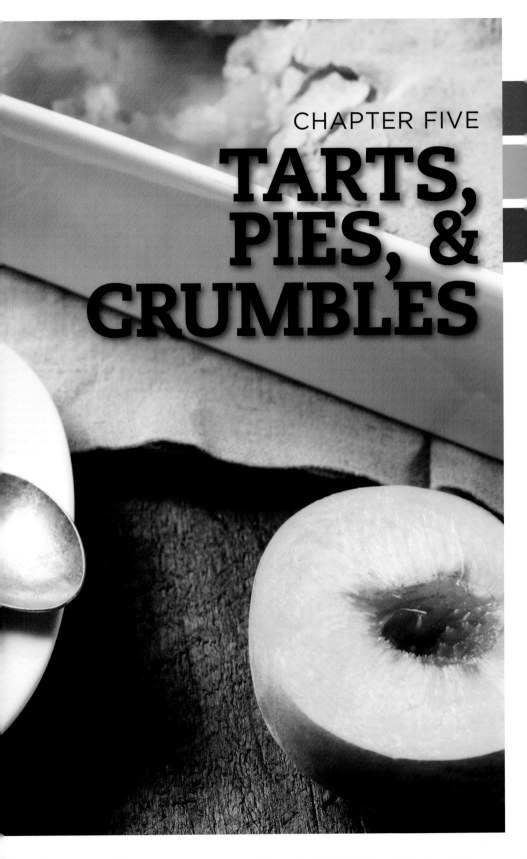

CHAPTER FIVE

TARTS, PIES, & CRUMBLES

Grilled Peaches with Honey & Cream

Why not grill your dessert too? Grilling caramelizes the fruit to create a dessert full of sweet flavors.

Prep time: 15 minutes   Cook time: 5 minutes   Makes 2 servings

2 peaches, pits removed, and cored

Cooking spray, for greasing

2 teaspoons brown sugar

Store-bought or homemade whipped cream (page 49) for serving

Honey, for serving

Mint, for serving (optional)

Preheat the grill to medium heat. Spray the inside of each peach with cooking spray. Place the peaches, cut-side down, onto the grill and cook until charred and tender, 5 to 6 minutes. Remove the peaches from the grill, sprinkle with brown sugar, and top with whipped cream, honey, and mint.

Berry Crumble

Bring on summer with this crumble! Swap out the mixed berries for any seasonal or frozen fruit.

Prep time: 15 minutes   Cook time: 25 minutes   Makes 2 servings

One 12-ounce bag frozen mixed berries

1 cup old-fashioned oats

¼ cup all-purpose flour

2 tablespoons brown sugar

2 tablespoons granulated sugar

½ teaspoon salt

4 tablespoons unsalted butter, chilled and diced

Vanilla ice cream or whipped cream (page 49), for serving

Preheat the oven to 350°F. Divide the berries between two 8-ounce ramekins or oven-proof mugs (if you don't have ramekins). Combine the remaining ingredients in a large bowl. Work the butter into the mixture using hands or the prongs of a fork until the butter resembles pea-sized pebbles. Divide the crumble evenly over the berries and place the ramekins on a baking sheet. Bake for 20 to 25 minutes, until the topping is golden brown and the fruit is warm and bubbling. Serve with a scoop of vanilla ice cream or dollop of whipped cream on top.

Cherry Hand Pies

Frozen berries and store-bought piecrust brings this dessert together quickly and easily.

Prep time: 15 minutes   Cook time: 20 minutes   Makes 4 pies

1 box store-bought pie dough

1½ cups frozen and thawed cherries

¼ cup granulated sugar plus additional for garnish

2 teaspoons cornstarch

1 tablespoon lemon juice

1 large egg, beaten

Preheat the oven to 350°F. Line a baking sheet with parchment paper. Using a 4-inch biscuit cutter, cut the piecrust into 8 rounds. Combine the cherries, sugar, cornstarch, and lemon juice. Divide the cherry mixture between 4 of the rounds. Top the cherry mixture with another pie dough round and seal the crust by pressing the prongs of a fork around the edges of each hand pie. Cut an X-shaped slit in the top of each pie. Place on the prepared baking sheet. Whisk the egg with 1 tablespoon of water. Brush the egg wash over the top of each hand pie. Sprinkle with sugar. Bake for 18 to 20 minutes, until the crust is golden and the filling is warmed through.

Peach Cobbler

Perfect to bake in advance for a picnic or small dinner party. Use your favorite seasonal or frozen fruit to make this classic dessert.

Prep time: 15 minutes   Cook time: 40 minutes   Makes 4 servings

Cooking spray, for greasing

One 14-ounce bag frozen sliced peaches, thawed

½ cup granulated sugar

1½ cups baking mix (such as Bisquick)

¾ cup milk

½ teaspoon ground cinnamon

5 tablespoons unsalted butter, melted

Vanilla ice cream, for serving

Preheat the oven to 375°F. Grease an 8-inch square baking dish with cooking spray. Stir together the peaches and sugar and pour into the prepared baking dish. In a seperate bowl, combine the baking mix, milk, cinnamon, and butter. Spread over the peaches. Bake for 35 to 40 minutes, until golden brown and cooked through. Allow to cool for 10 minutes and serve with ice cream.

Apple Plum Puff Pastry Tarts

Natural fruit sweetness shines in this dessert. Fruit on top of pillows of puff pastry creates a simple tart that will shine at the end of any meal.

Prep time: 15 minutes   Cook time: 30 minutes   Makes 4 tarts

1 cup apples, cored, and thinly sliced

2 plums, pitted, and thinly sliced

¼ cup granulated sugar

1 tablespoon lemon juice

1 sheet puff pastry

1 large egg

Store-bought or homemade whipped cream (page 49), for serving

Honey, for serving

Preheat the oven to 400°F. Line a baking sheet with parchment paper. Combine all the ingredients except for the puff pastry and honey and allow to macerate for 30 minutes. Cut the puff pastry into 4 squares. Score the puff pastry with a knife to form a ½-inch border. Whisk the egg and 1 tablespoon of water together. Brush the egg wash over the puff pastry. Bake for 12 to 15 minutes, until golden brown and puffed. Remove and allow to cool completely. Spoon the fruit over the top. Serve with whipped cream and a drizzle of honey.

Mini Chocolate Pecan Pies

Use a mini muffin tin for this recipe. Chocolate adds new decadence to traditional pecan pie.

Prep time: 25 minutes   **Cook time: 30 minutes**   **Makes 1 dozen mini pies**

Cooking spray, for greasing

1 sheet store-bought pie dough

2 tablespoons brown sugar

⅓ cup light corn syrup

1 large egg, beaten

½ teaspoon vanilla extract

½ cup pecans, roughly chopped

2 tablespoons mini chocolate chips

Preheat the oven to 350°F. Grease 12 wells of a mini muffin tin with cooking spray. Cut the piecrust into 12 small rounds with a 3-inch biscuit cutter and press into the mini muffin wells. Tuck the edges of the piecrust under if necessary. Combine the remaining ingredients in a large bowl. Divide the mixture between the mini piecrusts. Bake for 25 to 30 minutes, until the filling is set and the crust is golden brown. Remove from the oven to a baking rack to cool in the tin for 10 minutes. Remove the pies from the tin and allow to cool completely.

Apple Walnut Crumble

Bake in a baking dish or cast-iron skillet using your favorite apples in season.

Prep time: 20 minutes   Cook time: 45 minutes   Makes 4 servings

FOR THE APPLE FILLING

Cooking spray, for greasing

5 Honeycrisp apples, cored, and cut into ¼-inch slices

3 tablespoons brown sugar

½ teaspoon ground cinnamon

1 tablespoon all-purpose flour

Vanilla ice cream, for serving

FOR THE TOPPING

½ cup walnuts, roughly chopped

1½ cups old-fashioned oats

½ cup all-purpose flour

2 tablespoons brown sugar

4 tablespoons (½ stick) unsalted butter, chilled and diced

Preheat the oven to 350°F. Grease an 8-inch square baking dish with cooking spray. Combine the ingredients for the apple filling. Pour into the prepared baking dish. Combine the ingredients for the topping. Press the butter into the mixture using hands or the prongs of a fork until the butter forms pea-sized pieces. Spread the crumble mixture over the top of the apples. Bake for 40 to 45 minutes or until the crumble is golden brown and apples are cooked through. Cover with a piece of foil if topping is getting too dark. Allow to cool for 10 to 15 minutes and serve with vanilla ice cream.

Raspberry Almond Bars

These bars are great for a breakfast, lunch, or dinner treat. You can even pack them to enjoy at work or on the go.

Prep time: 15 minutes **Cook time: 40 minutes** **Makes 6 bars**

FOR THE BARS

Cooking spray, for greasing

2 cups baking mix (such as Bisquick)

¾ cup milk

½ teaspoon ground cinnamon

5 tablespoons unsalted butter, melted

1 cup raspberries or frozen and thawed raspberries

½ cup raspberry jam

1 tablespoon lemon juice

FOR THE TOPPING

1 cup old-fashioned oats

2 tablespoons brown sugar

½ cup almonds, roughly chopped

¼ cup all-purpose flour

3 tablespoons unsalted butter, chilled and diced

Preheat the oven to 350°F. Grease an 8-inch square baking dish with cooking spray. Combine baking mix, milk, cinnamon, and butter. Pour into the baking dish. Combine raspberries and jam and spread on top of the baking mix mixture. Combine the ingredients for the topping. Work the butter into the mixture using your hands or the prongs of a fork until the butter forms pea-sized pieces.

Spread the topping on top of the raspberries. Bake for 35 to 40 minutes until the crust is cooked through and the topping is golden brown. Remove from the oven and allow to cool on a baking rack. Slice and serve.

Peanut Butter Tartlets

These mini peanut butter treats are too easy to pop in your mouth, so make plenty—they will be gone in no time!

Prep time: 15 minutes   Cook time: 15 minutes
Makes 4 small tarts or 1 dozen mini tarts

Cooking spray, for greasing

½ roll of store-bought sugar cookie dough, softened

1 cup creamy peanut butter

1 to 2 tablespoons honey

¼ cup powdered sugar

½ cup semisweet chocolate chips

3 tablespoons heavy cream

Preheat the oven to 350°F. Grease 4 mini tart pans or a 12-well mini muffin tin with cooking spray. Place 1 to 2 tablespoons of sugar cookie dough into each cup and press the dough up the sides. Bake for 12 to 15 minutes, until the cookie is golden brown and cooked through. Remove from the oven to a baking rack and allow to cool completely. Meanwhile, combine the peanut butter, honey, and powdered sugar. If the peanut butter mixture is too thick, add a couple tablespoons of milk to thin it out. Place the mixture in a piping bag or zip-top bag with the corner cut off. Remove the cookie shells from the tin. Pipe the peanut butter mixture into the center of each cookie and smooth with an offset spatula or knife. Place the chocolate chips and heavy cream in a bowl and microwave at 15-second intervals, stirring until smooth. Spread over the top of the tarts. Allow to set.

Cranberry Apple Pie

This pie is made easily in a small cast-iron skillet. Just toss the ingredients together and bake!

Prep time: 15 minutes   Cook time: 25 minutes   Makes one 8-inch pie

Cooking spray, for greasing

2 small Gala apples, peeled, cored, and diced into ½-inch pieces

1½ cups frozen cranberries, thawed

½ cup granulated sugar

1 tablespoon all-purpose flour

2 tablespoons unsalted butter, cubed

1 store-bought round pie dough

1 large egg, beaten

1 tablespoon water

Preheat the oven to 375°F. Grease an 8-inch cast-iron pan with cooking spray. Combine the apples, cranberries, sugar, and flour in a large bowl. Pour into the cast-iron skillet and dot with butter. Place the piecrust on top and tuck in the edges. Mix the egg and 1 tablespoon water together and brush over the top of the piecrust. Cut three slits in the top of the piecrust. Bake for 20 to 25 minutes, until the piecrust is golden brown and the filling is cooked and bubbling. If piecrust is getting too brown during baking, shield with foil and continue to bake. Remove the pie from the oven and allow to cool for 10 minutes.

Caramel Nut Tartlets

Ooey and gooey chewy caramel tarts with a cookie crust—like a candy and a cookie, combined!

Prep time: 20 minutes   Cook time: 20 minutes   Makes 1 dozen mini tarts

Cooking spray, for greasing

½ roll store-bought sugar cookie dough

1¼ cups chewy caramels, unwrapped

3 tablespoons heavy cream

¼ cup pecans, chopped

¼ cup peanuts, chopped

1 teaspoon flaky sea salt

Preheat the oven to 350°F. Grease a mini muffin tin with cooking spray. Place 1 tablespoon of sugar cookie dough into each muffin well and press the dough up the sides. Bake for 10 to 12 minutes, until the cookie shells are golden brown and cooked through. Remove from the oven to a baking rack and allow to cool completely. Remove the cookie shells from the muffin tin. Meanwhile, in a microwave-safe bowl, microwave the caramels at 15-second intervals, stirring, until smooth. When smooth, add the heavy cream and whisk to combine. Evenly sprinkle the chopped nuts into the bottom of each cookie shell, top with the melted caramel mixture, and sprinkle with sea salt. Allow to set.

Index